This book is written for all children to enjoy and
to learn about their family history, especially travelling children
and the children of Deptford, South London

For the historical background to this children's book please see
'Deptford Show Ground: the last permanent fairground in London', by Angela Catherine Cain
published in 2022 by Grosvenor House Publishing Ltd.

Contact: 07837938321
Angela Catherine Cain
andriacfalk@yahoo.com

Magic in Deptford

Angela Catherine Cain

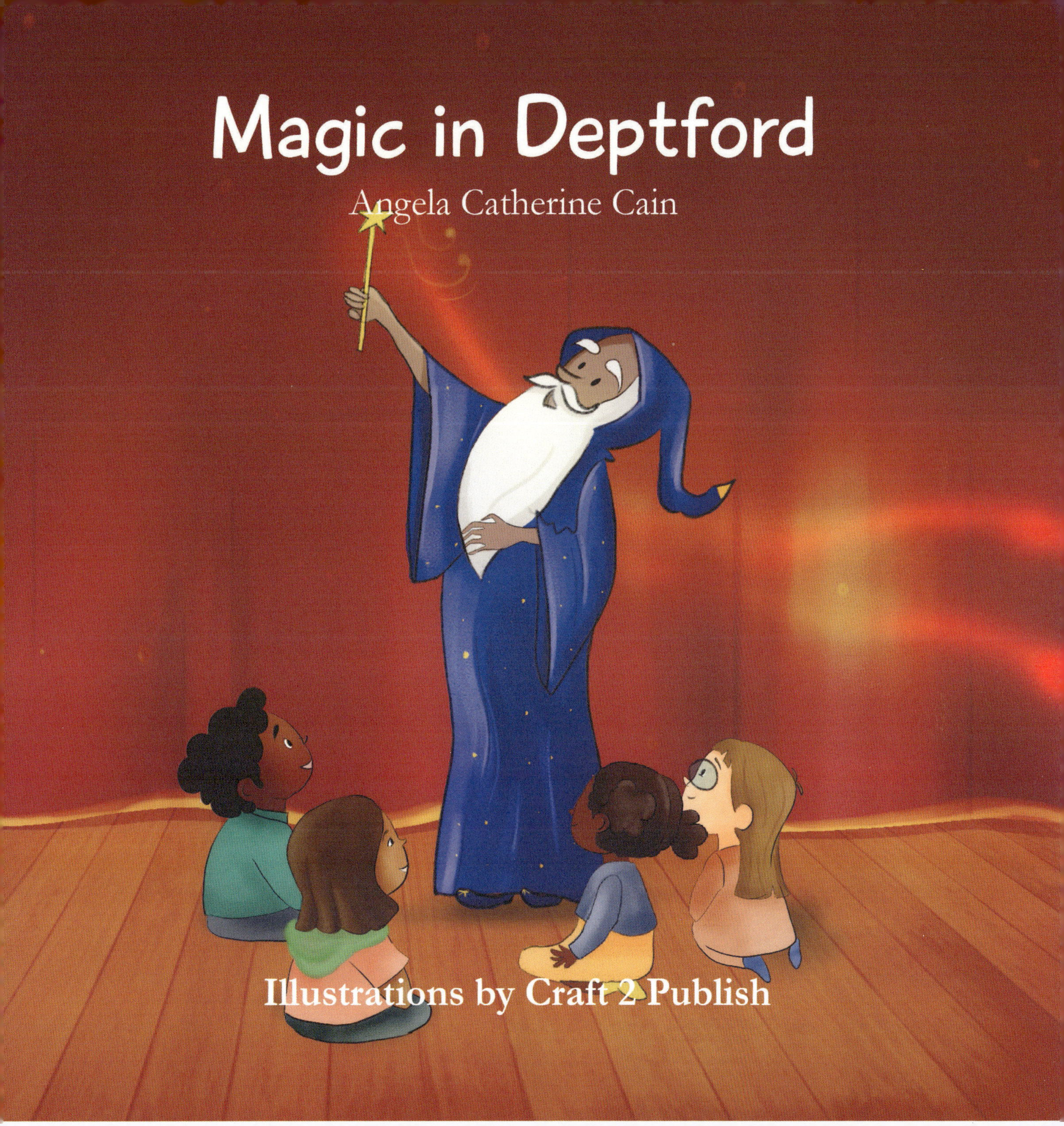

Illustrations by Craft 2 Publish

Hello, I'm a magician. My name is Giffin. I live in Deptford, South London.

I'm going to tell you a true story about Deptford that only a few people know about.

I have a special magic wand that makes me into a time traveller.
This means I can go back and forwards in time.

Hocus pocus, Giffin focus
Back in time! With this rhyme!
Abracadabra ... Wh-o-o-sh!

I'm a bit rusty. I need to practise.

Will you help me?

Hocus pocus, Giffin focus
Back in time! With this rhyme!
Abracadabra ... Wh-o-o-sh!

Yes, the magic works! Now, what can we see.....

This is how my friends Charles and Hannah lived when they first came to Deptford.

They slept in their wagon and their children slept in a tent.
Their horse pulled their wagon all the way to Deptford from the countryside.
It was a long way...

...and it was a long time ago, over a hundred and thirty years ago.

This is what Charles and Hannah looked like when they came to Deptford. They were wearing their best clothes. They liked Deptford because it was an easier life and they didn't have to travel around all the time.

Let's see why Charles and Hannah decided to come to Deptford.

Hocus pocus, Giffin focus
Back in time! With this rhyme!

Abracadabra ... Wh-o-o-sh!

Ah Yes. Charles and Hannah were showmen, bringing their travelling fun fair to Deptford.

In those days, there were wild animal shows on the fairground.

They had all sorts of animals: camels, lions, elephants and even a zebra.

Is that a lion?

Yes, his name is Wallace.

He doesn't look too happy to me. What do you think?

There was a travelling cinema on the fairground in Deptford.
They called it a 'cinematograph'.

In those days, to see a film you had to go to the fair.

The cinematograph came to Deptford on a trailer pulled by a steam engine like this one.

Is that a boxing show?

Oh yes! You could test your strength against the boxers who worked on the fairground and win a prize.

Charles and Hannah had big ideas and needed a lot of money.

They sold 'swag' to their friends on different fairgrounds:
toys and knick-knacks to use as prizes.

'Swag'

And they made lots and lots of money!

They made so much money that they were able to build a big house on the fairground for their family.

They also built a big warehouse for the 'swag'.
Here is Charles in front of the warehouse.

Then, they had enough money to buy a big carousel.

Can you see Carrie? Her job was to collect the money.

When the fair was closed, Hannah dried her washing on the carousel.

The whole family was needed to work on the fairground.

This is Charles and Hannah with their eight children: David, Tom, Fred and Charlie, at the back and Hannah, Daisy, Florence and Carrie at the front. Do you like their fancy hats?

They sold so much 'swag' that they needed to buy a big lorry to take it to other fairs.

This is how the fairground looked from up high.

Can you see the fairground house and the warehouse in the background?
And the fairground rides in the middle?

In the winter, lots of different showmen came to Deptford with their rides. Baileys brought their ark and their skid. And Irvins brought their helter-skelter.

'Ark'

'Skid'

'Helter Skelter'

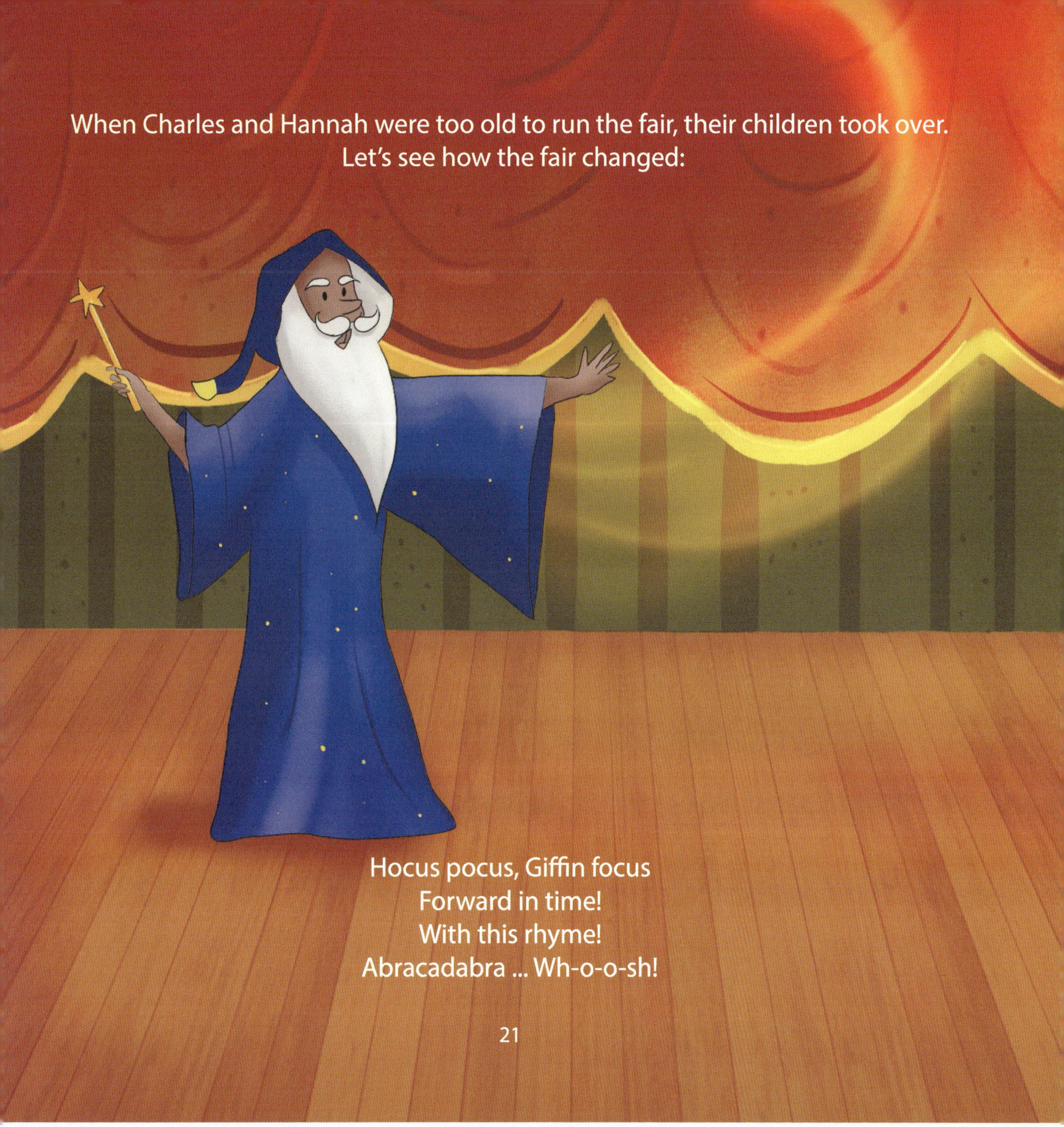

When Charles and Hannah were too old to run the fair, their children took over. Let's see how the fair changed:

Hocus pocus, Giffin focus
Forward in time!
With this rhyme!
Abracadabra ... Wh-o-o-sh!

The children decided the roundabout was too slow...
and the games were too old,
so they decided to buy some dodgems.

And they built a wall-of-death ride with motorbikes that spun around a track.

There were new swing boats that everyone enjoyed.

There was a big punch ball. You could pay one old penny to have a go and see how strong you were.

Over 60 years ago in 1961, everyone was very sad because the fairground closed down.
This is how the closure of the showground was reported in the newspaper:

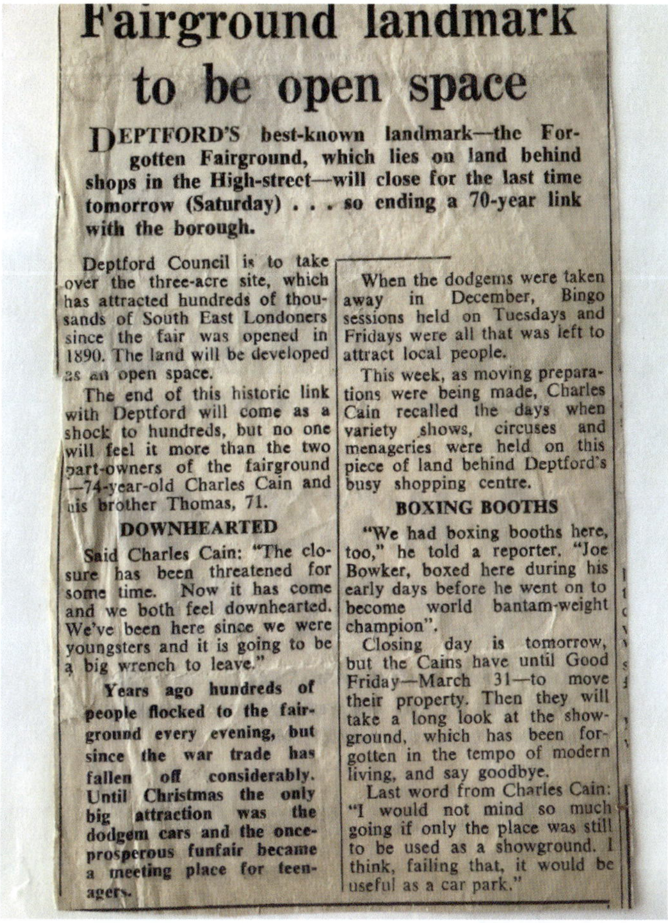

Fairground landmark to be open space

DEPTFORD'S best-known landmark—the Forgotten Fairground, which lies on land behind shops in the High-street—will close for the last time tomorrow (Saturday) . . . so ending a 70-year link with the borough.

Deptford Council is to take over the three-acre site, which has attracted hundreds of thousands of South East Londoners since the fair was opened in 1890. The land will be developed as an open space.

The end of this historic link with Deptford will come as a shock to hundreds, but no one will feel it more than the two part-owners of the fairground —74-year-old Charles Cain and his brother Thomas, 71.

DOWNHEARTED

Said Charles Cain: "The closure has been threatened for some time. Now it has come and we both feel downhearted. We've been here since we were youngsters and it is going to be a big wrench to leave."

Years ago hundreds of people flocked to the fairground every evening, but since the war trade has fallen off considerably. Until Christmas the only big attraction was the dodgem cars and the once-prosperous funfair became a meeting place for teenagers.

When the dodgems were taken away in December, Bingo sessions held on Tuesdays and Fridays were all that was left to attract local people.

This week, as moving preparations were being made, Charles Cain recalled the days when variety shows, circuses and menageries were held on this piece of land behind Deptford's busy shopping centre.

BOXING BOOTHS

"We had boxing booths here, too," he told a reporter. "Joe Bowker, boxed here during his early days before he went on to become world bantam-weight champion".

Closing day is tomorrow, but the Cains have until Good Friday—March 31—to move their property. Then they will take a long look at the showground, which has been forgotten in the tempo of modern living, and say goodbye.

Last word from Charles Cain: "I would not mind so much going if only the place was still to be used as a showground. I think, failing that, it would be useful as a car park."

After that, the old fairground became a car park and dumping ground, which made me sad.

But then I was happy because Deptford Council decided to build a library and a school on the old fairground.

Let's have a look at the school and the library.

Hocus pocus, Giffin focus
Forward in time. With this rhyme
Abracadabra ... Whoosh!

Here's a photo of the library...

...and here's the children's library.

Have a good look at the photo. Charles and Hannah's old house on the fairground is now part of the school

...and here's the school. Can you see its name?
Yes, Tidemill Academy

I wonder what's different about it?

And this is the old warehouse on the fairground.
Once upon a time, it was full of fairground prizes.
Now it's full of children and teachers.

Isn't that a-m-a-z-i-n-g!

Here are Francesca and David, great grandchildren of Charles and Hannah's, with their cousin.
They like to remember the old fairground in Deptford.

Bye! Have a good day!

When you want to remember things going back and forwards in time you can time travel and call on Giffin to help you.

You could even try making a magic wand!

Hocus pocus, Giffin focus
Back in time! With this rhyme!
Abracadabra ... Wh-o-o-sh!

New words for you to learn

An ark. This is a fairground ride with motor bikes, benches or animals that go up and down and round-and-round, see page 19.

A carousel is another name for a roundabout, see page 15.

A cinematograph is a mobile cinema that first started on the fairground over a 150 years ago, before there were buildings where you could see a film, see page 9.

Dodgems. This is a fairground ride with small electric cars to be dodged or bumped into, see page 22.

A helter skelter is shaped like an upside-down ice cream cone and has a slide that twists around the outside, see page 20.

Showmen. People whose job and responsibility is to be in charge of fairgrounds, see page 7.

A skid. A fairground ride with spinning cars that go round and round and up and down, see page 20.

Steam engine. Before cars and lorries were invented, steam engines were used that relied on coal to make energy and pull fairground rides and other heavy objects around, page 10.

Swag. Prizes to be won on the fairground, see page 12.

A wagon is a big caravan that showmen live in and travel to different fairgrounds, see page 3.

Wall of death. An old fairground ride with motor cycles ridden around a wooden track, see page 22.

Photographs. Please note these photographs may only be reprinted with permission of the author or an appropriate commercial or other organisation. Page 3 and 4 ©Bell family archive, page 6A ©Harry Cox, Vale of Health, page 6B Courtesy of the Fairground Society, page 7 National Fairground and Circus Archive, page 8 postcard 'Wallace at Purchases Menagerie' Shutterstock/Chris Doney, page 9, courtesy of Ricky Manley, page 10 courtesy of the Fairground Society, page 11 courtesy of the Fairground Society, page 13A courtesy of Alison Flatt, Page 13B Dreamstime, page 12, 14-18 ©Bell family archive, page 19 ©Jack Leeson/National Fairground and Circus Archive, page 20A ©Michael A. Smith/ National Fairground and Circus Archive, page 20B, ©Irvin family archive, page 22A Pinterest, page 22B ©Irvin family archive, page 23 National Fairground and Circus Archive, page 24A Dreamstime, page 24B courtesy of James Anthony Mcdaid, page 25 Kentish Mercury 1961, page 27A © Pollard, Thomas and Edwards Architects, photographer Robert Greshoff, 27B, 28-29 ©Cain family archive, page 30 ©Family archive David Cain Senior. Back cover family archive and Pinterest.

Printed in Dunstable, United Kingdom

67961893R00022